birdies

How To Tell a Duck Hooker
From a Deep-Rough Thrasher

GOLFING BIRDS ENTERPRISES,INC.™

By Roy Benjamin

Illustrations by Oscar

96 95 94 93 92   10 9 8 7 6 5 4 3 2 1

Produced and published by: Golfing Birds Enterprises, Inc.
Design: Leonard P. Leone

ISBN 0-9633960-0-5

Bulk quantities of BIRDIES are available at special discounts for use by companies and
organizations in gift, premium, public relations and marketing programs. For information
on discounts and special customizing featuring a sponsor's message and identification
on the back cover, contact the publisher.

GOLFING BIRDS ENTERPRISES, INC.
21 DUPONT AVENUE
WHITE PLAINS, NY 10605
PHONE: (914) 949-5107 or (800) 735-BIRD
FAX: (914) 997-7214

INTRODUCTION
by
BOB HOPE

Fellow golfers, don't these birds remind you of the people you play with? My friend Dinah Shore is certainly a *Sweet Swinging Swallow*, and *The Surveyor Stork* made me think of my old golfing pal Perry Como. He once took so long over a putt that the green grew into rough.

One of golf's real characters and great champions, Jimmy Demaret, once said "Bob Hope has a great short game. Unfortunately it's off the tee."

I've played for fifty-five years and my handicap today is 20, although at one time I was down to six. However, I still love the game as much as ever, because very early on I discovered its secret: *swing with a sense of humor.* That's what these hilarious golfing birdies are doing, and I hope you do too.

I also hope we all get to play a lot with *The Big-Hearted Pigeon* and can always avoid *The Shanking Spoonbill* and *The Ear-Bending Crow*.

In keeping with the style of author Roy Benjamin may I close with:

> You've a real treat in store in this birdie-watching book.
> You'll find partners and friends (and an occasional crook).
> From the fairways and greens to the blue skies above
> We can say without pause: *Golf's a game we all love!*

C⦾NTENTS

FEATHERED
FRIENDS,
FOES
AND
FOIBLES

The Big-Hearted Pigeon

Our Pigeon never wins a bet.
He just pays off. He doesn't fret.
We love his three putts (and his wealth).
Dear Lord, please keep him in good health!

The Scrambling Falcon

This Falcon has a special flair
For hitting shots we'd never dare.
Although his scrambles are bizarre,
He always seems to get his par.

The Ruffle-Feathered Grouse

The golfing Grouse is a chronic complainer.
He's harder to take than a total abstainer.
He rants and he raves when his shots go askew.
He's constantly moaning, 'cause most of them do.

The Schizophrenic Gull

The Gull is at the practice range.
His swing is grooved and strong.
His perfect timing doesn't change.
Each shot is straight and long.
But when he tees it up to play,
His game evaporates.
Each ball he hits now goes astray,
And par fours turn to eights.
This gull who practiced like an ace
Plays like a bobolink.
He's now become a basket case,
And needs to see a shrink.

The Sweet-Swinging Swallow

The Swallow's swing is sweet as honey.
That's why she's always in the money.
Smooth, unhurried, tempo great,
She hits a ball that's long and straight.

The Sandbagging Vulture

This Vulture's joy is to win if it kills.
(With a handicap phony as three-dollar bills.)
He sets a sly trap, and if you take the bait,
He'll play *his* true game, and *you'll* pay the freight.

The Surveyor Stork

The Surveyor Stork, to achieve his mission,
Thinks he must take up a prone position.
He measures, he plumbs, he cubes and squares.
He mutters and moans while his foursome swears.
He squints and he squats – "My God, what a bore!"
Then he misses his putt by two feet or more.

The O.O.B. Turkey

This Turkey's drive has a flight that's non-sensical –
Not just out of bounds, but over the fence-ical.

The Very Heavy Albatross

The mariner stood upon the deck,
An Albatross wrapped 'round his neck.
Think of him when it's your fate
To drag your partner's heavy weight.

The Short-Fused Kite

Drive's no good,
Slams his wood.

In a creek,
Swears a streak.

Next tough lie,
Goes sky high.

Putt's elusive,
Gets abusive.

Shot's a dub,
Throws his club.

Starts to lose,
Blows a fuse.

In a ditch,
"Son of a #✔❋✗❢"

Kite's a menace.
Should play tennis!

The Multihued Chickadee

The Multihued Chickadee gives not a hoot
For the horrible scores she will manage to shoot.
Her primary goal, her desire, her passion,
Is to dazzle her friends with the latest in fashion.

The Ear-Bending Crow

Avoid at all cost the Ear-Bending Crow.
He'll describe every shot from the very first go.
Every drive, every putt, every hook, every slice,
(And if you're not listening, he'll run through it twice).
The way to escape this loud-crowing bore
Is to say at the start, "Just tell me your score."

The Links Maven Raven

Have you heard of a maven named Raven?
Golf to him is a passionate cravin'.
From the dawn's early light
He'll keep playing 'til night.
Squawks his spouse . . . "This match ain't worth savin'."

The Debt-Defying Darter

The Darter likes to win all bets.
(He also hates to pay his debts.)
He darts and dips with explanations
Why he can't meet his obligations.
"Can you change a hundred?" "My wallet is lost."
"I'll see you next week." "Just fax me the cost."
Before you tee off, you should let this bird know
You want a deposit in feathered escrow.

The Dawdling Creeper

The Dawdling Creeper is a bird we should nail.
He plods down the course with the pace of a snail.
He also seems deaf; you can yell 'til you're blue:
"Two holes are wide open. Please let us play through!"

The Racing Roadrunner

The Roadrunner sets a very fast pace.
Golf for him is an eighteen-hole race.
At the end of a round when asked "What's your score?"
He proudly reports: "Three hours and four."

The Needling Snipe

The Snipe is as subtle as a kick in the rear.
He sounds like a friend but he plays on your fear.
He warns, "Don't be scared by that very small lake."
"Forget your last shank and watch that out-of-bounds stake."
He speaks with a smile but he hopes he can get you
With negative thoughts that are meant to upset you.

The White-Whiskered Coot

Don't challenge the Coot to a match.
Beware of that eye with the patch.
He's not fit as a fiddle,
But he drives down the middle
And drops every putt down the hatch.

The Alibi Shrike

"That bounce was unfair." "The ball just won't 'sit.' "
"My club must have slipped." "You talked as I hit."
"The greens are too slow." "The rough is too long."
"The traps have no sand." "The wind is too strong."
The Alibi Shrike has excuses galore
For missing a shot or failing to score.
The game that he plays is "I woulda or coulda."
Better this bird in his bed "shoulda stooda."

The Dainty Divot Dove

A paragon of virtue is the Dainty Divot Dove.
She tidies up the golf course with an all-consuming love.
Each ball mark is an insult to our lady of the links;
Each divot is a bloody wound. "Alas, for shame,"
    she thinks.
And footprints in the sands of traps, "Oh dear,
    for goodness' sake!"
Her motto is the golfer's creed: Repair, Replace
    and Rake!

The Crafty Counting Hawk

The score card of this Hawk is trim.
The strokes add up . . . but not for him.
With crafty counting, he'll contrive
To turn a seven into a five.

The Shanking Spoonbill

Don't look at the Spoonbill who shanks.
When he asks you to play, say "No, thanks."
If you watch this poor bird's affliction
You'll learn it can be an addiction.
For shanks are not only outrageous;
They become completely contagious.

The Scottish Storm Petrel

The Scottish Storm Petrel finds golf's greatest pleasure
Is battling the elements, measure for measure.
"If nae winds and nae rain, it's nae golf" is his lore.
When it's calm and there's sunshine, the game is a bore.

The Huffin' Puffin

An overweight bird is this portly Puffin.
Which goes to explain why he's always huffin'.
His poundage is awesome; his belly's a pot.
That's why he rides in his golf cart a lot.

The "Gimme"-Taking Lark

This Lark thinks a "gimme" is his lawful due.
He'll take that three-footer before you say "Boo".
But when it's *your* ball that could be in doubt,
He's quick to tell you, "Hey, just putt it out."

The Waggling Woodpecker

Back and forth and forth and back and
    back and forth he goes.
He can't get off his grounded heels or
    on his twitching toes.
His wiggle waggles are a stall.
He's really scared to hit the ball.
His partners plead, "Get off the mark!
Or else we'll finish after dark."

The Flightless Emu

Come winter, summer, spring, or fall,
The Emu never hits a ball.
He'd rather read than test his skills
On close-cut greens or bunkered hills.
Instead of on the practice tees,
From books he gains his expertise.
He'll spend all day with *Golf Digest,*
But never in golf clubs invest.
He's first to tell us what is wrong:
"Your swing's too short." "Your grip's too strong."
An armchair master is this guy.
To him we say, "Why don't you fly?"

The Septuagenarian Rooster

Observe the Septuagenarian Rooster.
He wishes he could swing like he used-ter.

The Cocky Catbird

The Catbird says, "This game is a breeze;
Watch me bring this course to its knees."
On the very next hole he develops a hook.
Then he hits in the woods and from there to the brook.
The sport is a breeze if sailing's your game.
In golf it's not "cocky" but "humble" 's the name.

The Rule-Breaking Mockingbird

He makes a mockery of the rules.
Those who obey, he says, are fools.
He has no fear of traps or rough;
A kick, a nudge . . . *his* lie's not tough.

The Migrating Geese

The Migrating Geese keep an eye out for snow.
At the very first flake they pack up and go
To Phoenix, La Costa or Boca Raton,
Callaway Gardens or sunny San Juan.
Bermuda, Palm Desert or to Key Biscayne,
Jamaica, La Quinta, Soto Grande in Spain.
They fly to hot spots where the sun shines
   the most –
New Mexico's desert or Florida's coast.
Though the golfing's great, how long can you
   roam?
These Geese return honking: "There's no
   course like home."

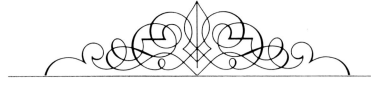

STROKE-SAVING TIPS STRAIGHT FROM THE PENGUIN PROS

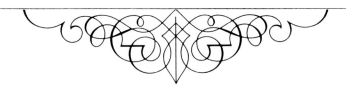

The Penguin Pros

Visit your pros if your back swing's not slow.
They'll reveal why you're scuffing the ball off the toe.
They'll stop you from gripping the club much too tight
And show how to give an approach shot some height.

Turn straight to the source if you feel your game slipping.
They'll smartly disclose why your putter keeps yipping.
When your drives are mere dribbles and your club
   tops the ball,
They'll take your game in for a quick overhaul.

These Penguins know how to give great direction.
They'll explain how to hone your game to perfection.
They're healers and helpers and friends and confessors.
As PGA members, they're your own golf professors.

The Duck Hooker

This hooker hits a ball that ducks,
Inspiring cuss words worse than "shucks."
He must stop his roundhouse wheeling,
And get that "hands to target" feeling!

The Reckless Loon

The Reckless Loon from impossible spots,
Will foolishly try ridiculous shots.
Instead of taking a penalty stroke
Or the rule of unplayable lies invoke,
Our Loon will hit from inside a ditch
Or out of the water attempt to pitch.
He cares not a whit that he nicks his clubs,
That most of his tries are spectacular flubs.
Although we all love an optimist,
We've put this bird on our stupid list.

The Reluctant Tern

An aptly named bird is the Tern,
Because that's what we all should learn.
Forget useless tips,
Just swivel your hips.
Remember the Tern when you turn.

The Flicking Flicker

A bird who hesitates to swing
Will not a song of triumph sing.
So . . . Flicking Flicker heed this call,
"Turn on your strength. Hit *through* the ball!"

The Quivering Quail

When this Quivering Quail puts his ball in a bunker,
He's quailing with fear that he'll next hit a clunker.
But there is no cause to be scared of a trap.
Just follow these tips and the shot is a snap:
Keep your stance and the face of your club opened wide;
Hit three inches behind and from the "outside."
And also, please take this hint as your clue:
Your head must stay down, with hands swinging through.

The Deep-Rough Thrasher

The Thrasher's words are thoroughly rash.
"I'll beat this deep rough with a bang and a bash."
Now is the time he should use his thick head,
And play the ball safe . . . or else he'll be dead.

The Wise Auld Owl

He was there when the game of golf began.
He belongs to Tom Morris's ancient clan.
So he's solved the riddle of golf, it's said.
"Think, laddies, of only your hands and your head.
"The answer," he whispers as he drifts through the mists,
" 'Tis above your neck and below your wrists."

The Chicken-Hearted Putter

A putter with a chicken heart
Will seldom play the champion's part.
To hole the ball and claim the win,
Say "Never up, it's never in."

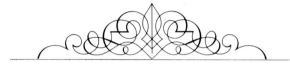

THE
WING AND FOOT
GOLF CLUB

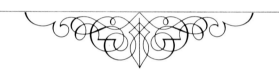

ABOUT THE AUTHOR

Roy Benjamin has written numerous articles on golf and other subjects and is co-author of the best-selling instruction book, *The Golfer's Stroke-Saving Handbook* (Little, Brown and Company).

He is also a twelve-time club champion of Fairview Country Club, Greenwich, CT.

Mr. Benjamin lives in White Plains, N.Y., where he is chairman of The Benjamin Company, book publishers, which he founded with his brother, Ted, in 1953.

The idea for *BIRDIES* came to the author while playing golf with a Big-Hearted Pigeon and a Ruffle-Feathered Grouse, behind a foursome of Dawdling Creepers.

ABOUT THE ILLUSTRATOR

Oscar is the nom de plume of an artist who made these illustrations for a lark.

FOR ADDITIONAL COPIES

To order additional copies of *BIRDIES - How to Tell a Duck Hooker from a Deep-Rough Thrasher,* visit your local bookseller or, if unavailable, use this page to order directly from the publisher at the following prices.

Single copy: @ $19.95 plus $3.00 postage and handling
2 to 9 copies: @ $19.95 plus $1.50 postage and handling
10 to 24 copies: @ $19.95. We pay postage and handling
25 to 49 copies: @ $17.95. We pay postage and handling
50 to 99 copies: @ $16.95. We pay postage and handling

For 100 or more copies for use as gifts, prizes,
or in premium, marketing or public relations programs,
write, fax, or phone for special discounts.

ORDER FORM

Publisher: **GOLFING BIRDS ENTERPRISES, INC.**
21 Dupont Avenue, White Plains, NY 10605
Phone: (914) 949-5107 or (800) 735-BIRD
Fax: (914) 997-7214

Please send me _____ copies of BIRDIES @ $ _____ per copy.

Check for $ _____ enclosed. (NY, NJ, California residents, please add appropriate sales tax.)

Charge: ☐ American Express; ☐ Visa; ☐ MasterCard

Card #_____ Expiration _____

(PLEASE PRINT)

Name _____

Company _____ Title _____

Address _____ Phone (_____) _____

City _____ State _____ ZIP_____

Signature _____

OTHER "BIRDIES" ITEMS

Please write the publisher if you would like information on such BIRDIES items as Appointment Books; Calendars; Ceramic Figures; Cocktail Napkins; Coffee Mugs; Desk Diaries; Greeting Cards; Laminated Plaques; Place Mats; Posters; or T-Shirts.